Poetry from a Road Scholar

Poetry from a Road Scholar

James Robert Murphy

Foreword by Mary Jo Melby

RESOURCE *Publications* · Eugene, Oregon

POETRY FROM A ROAD SCHOLAR

Resource Publications
An Imprint of Wipf and Stock Publishers
199 W. 8th Ave., Suite 3
Eugene, OR 97401

www.wipfandstock.com

PAPERBACK ISBN: 978-1-7252-6540-0
HARDCOVER ISBN: 978-1-7252-6539-4
EBOOK ISBN: 978-1-7252-6541-7

Manufactured in the U.S.A.   03/24/20

Thank you Margarita and Ian. You are the world to me.
Thank you to my good friends Mary Jo Melby, Jay Duncan,
Richard and Cristina Palmer, and Katherine Brennand.
Your time and attention is invaluable.

Thank you Margarita and Ian. You are the world to me.
Thank you to my good friends Mary Jo Melby, Jay Duncan,
Richard and Cristina Palmer, and Katherine Brennand.
Your time and attention is invaluable.

Contents

Foreword

JAMES ROBERT (JIM) MURPHY is a Renaissance Man. The term "Renaissance Man" has been defined as a person with many talents or areas of knowledge. Jim certainly epitomizes this description. He is a poet, yes, but also a songwriter, a painter, has authored five books, plays guitar and sings—solo and with a variety of musical groupings.

But what makes a true Renaissance Man goes way beyond just possessing the aforementioned talents. It takes tenacity—putting your assets into action. Jim does this. He jumps into life at the moment of inspiration and just paints or sings or writes. While many talented people think about creating, Jim creates.

Coming from a youth filled with adventure and sometimes even danger, Jim writes from the heart and experiences. I believe that many of us would agree that it's when we are in those formative young years that emotions are felt so deeply. Because Jim kept journals during much of his life he is able to recall so many of his feelings in a very real way.

Poetry from a Road Scholar reminds us of the close way in which all of the arts are connected. We see the conductor leading his orchestra while visualizing different colors and the artist painting to the inspiration of his favorite music. Magical!!

Sit back and enjoy the fun as Jim Murphy takes us to places only a poet such as he can travel.

Mary Jo Melby
Past President,
El Paso Chapter of the
National Society of Arts and Letters

Introduction

WHEN I WAS A youth living hand-to-mouth on the road, life was not easy by any means. While others in my small town of 2,200 residents found steady work or went to college, I chose to make my way day by day hitchhiking from town to town and state to state. The one thing I never did was beg on a street corner or ask for a handout. Raised as a carpenter from the time I was twelve, framing homes in Texas, and condominiums in the mountains of Colorado paid the fare at times. Washing dishes for nights in a row would also provide meals and money to continue traveling. Playing music for meals and tips in Oregon, and picking apples in Chelan, Washington for thirty straight days granted shelter, money and the opportunity to work alongside Mexican migrants. Nothing came easy. This lifestyle, while dangerous and insecure, did furnish imagery for song and poetry. I lived by these means for more than a decade.

While not my first intent, *Poetry from a Road Scholar* is a chapter by chapter, relationship by relationship poetic storyline. I first thought of placing the pieces in the order in which they were written. Almost immediately this seemed to provide no coherency at all. The randomness of writing doesn't necessarily conform to a logical storyline. I then considered organizing my work by year to create some sort of an annual theme. This did not work either. And then I decided to create relationship storylines based on the poems themselves. That being said, apparently, I've been in fourteen relationships. Looking back, that might be about right.

When I began to earnestly put this project together I conducted a thorough search through my seventeen travel logs that led to the rediscovery of nearly 900 partial and completed songs, stories, letters to friends and loved ones never sent, plans for videos that could never afford to be produced, and a few ragged sketches of myself and my on-the-road compadres. Of course, I'd gone through my logs hundreds of times over the years searching for one thing or another, but never in this much detail.

Once I had cataloged when the text was written and I actually studied the text, I realized that I was just a teenager and in my early twenties when the great majority of these works had been penned. I was pleasantly surprised by the somber words woven together that spoke truth in every phrase. Writing, whether we'd like it to be or not, is all about the truth. *Poetry from a Road Scholar* points to a repeated history of human yearning. The wanting need to be with someone, the sincere beginnings followed by the attempts at reconciliation and the angry pissedoffidness that follows each failed attempt. Some works are humorous, some are sprinkled with sexual overtones, some are deep and perhaps even philosophical. Most are in plain English written by a young man from Upstate New York.

The phrase *Road Scholar* was born out of this one particularly quirky memory I recalled while reminiscing. Somewhere along the way, in my late teens while on the road in Colorado, I had heard on the radio that Kris Kristofferson was a Road Scholar. How interesting I thought, that he and I were both educated by our travels on the road. From that point on I always believed Kris and I were one in the same. I never bragged about it but I was very proud of that little tidbit. It wasn't until years later that I 'read' Mr. Kristofferson was a *Rhodes Scholar* and not a *Road Scholar*. I'd never heard of a Rhodes Scholar before. After exploring what a Rhodes Scholar is, I realized that Kris and I weren't by any means traveling up and down the same roads. Be that as it may, I still believe Kris and I are some sort of kindred spirits.

I

Fireside Lullaby

Seems like the road
is my only friend
Seems like the road
it never ends

I'm just looking for a woman
to keep me warm
on those cold, cold nights

Seems like the sun
is all I need for life
Seems like the stars
tell a fine lullaby at night

I'm just looking for a woman
to be my friend
for all time

I listened to the ocean
and it sounds just like the wind
I made a new life in the mountains
and I'll be back there when I can

I'm just looking for a woman
who doesn't need
life's finer things

Little Does She Know

Little does she know
she's in love with a man who enjoys his sorrow
Feeling as though it's better to be alone

Once again she comes wandering
down the walkway into my life
Touching my hand she turns the stone to water

I can talk like a young boy
who needs the care she offers
living in a house with so many rooms

Please tell me if you are a friend of mine
it will hurt me not to see you when the morning comes
For I too have been looking for someone to be free with
and whatever your life brings to you
I shall not come between

Little do I know
I'm in love with a woman who enjoys her sorrow
Seeing it through a better change in time

I know that if I please to
I can be alone
For a day
into a week
sure signs of more

There's a candle burning close to me
as the moon fills the canyon
and I see myself
in a place where I have never been

Let the light in brother
you know you're just running scared
She is the bouquet of flowers that sets upon your table
and the reason you laugh
when you just said something you did not mean

Let the light in brother
you know you've got something to share
It takes so long to end that chain of misery
in-between

Little do you know
you're in love with a friend who will soothe your sorrows
The feeling is so much better when you are the one

There's a still life to be gazed upon
as the sun speaks with your garden
and the river travels swiftly under our window

I have met the ways of barroom courtships
and have heard when love comes to my door
I will know
I will know
I heard you knocking
and felt the wind upon my face

No Count Outlaw

I get up in the morning
look into the mirror
Lines on my face
are looking so much clearer
I walk into the bedroom
I see you lying there
an angel from heaven
what's she doing here

I'm a no-count outlaw
blood stains on my hands
a life spent behind bars
a liar and a thief

Just before I leave
to face the working day
I sit down on the bed beside her
not knowing what to say
She slowly opens up her eyes
and smiles within her heart
She whispers that she loves me
and would I kiss her 'for I part

I'm a no-count outlaw
vengeance used for blood
Why in the world would a pretty girl
be giving me her love

As I gently kiss her
warm and tender lips
A feeling comes over me
of love and tenderness

Maybe this angel
sent from up above
can fill this heart of stone
with something known as love

I'm a no-count outlaw
blood stains on my hands
a life spent behind bars
a liar and a thief

I'm a no-count outlaw
vengeance used for blood
Why in the world would a pretty girl
be giving me her love
Why in the world would a pretty girl
be giving me her love

Why in the world

would a pretty girl

be giving me

her love

Riding on a Wave

I'm riding on a wave
that's forcing blue to white
seeing what this life will bring to me

Feeling like I've broken
the patterns from which I've grown
looking back I see I was alone

I have been a migrant
a fisher of the seas
surprised to find this is a life of luxury

Flowers in the desert
snow upon the mountains
I lay upon the soil
it turns to grey

I'm sorry I cannot tell you
I've tried and tried again
I've spent the time allotted
now I must go

It's not the wind that's calling me
it's not a path I follow
but some restless river
flowing from the moon

I've shaken hands with the pretender
under the watchful eye of his brother
laughing through a mask I wore so well

Shaken by the tremor
that pulled upon my heartstrings
I knew I must not choose the beaten path

Two Flames Burning

There's two flames burning
one is in my heart for you

There's two flames burning
both of them can see us through

One is the fire in my heart
the other is the fire in your heart

There's two flames burning
both of them can see us through

Day of the Buffalo

Sittin' here and I'm stoned again
but I'm feelin' pretty good
It's almost a full moon outside
and old man winter's at the door

Truck's got a flat, I ain't been paid in a month
There's bruises on my woman's arms
I wish my thumb was the pilot it used to be
For some reason
I think I need more

Bring me back to the day of the buffalo
Back before days of millions
Let me rest my head on your shoulder
for I feel like I'm fixin' to cry

Old Tom he'll be in Vermont soon
you should hear him play that old mandolin
Tom Coates he's with a lady of the canyon
and Hoag Tyler a son to the redwoods

I remember the Verde Hot Springs
I was so high I almost took off
Now I'm back in the city
and I question myself every day

Bring me back to the day of the buffalo
Back before days of millions
Let me rest my head on your shoulder
for I feel like I'm fixin' to cry
for I feel like I'm fixin' to cry
I'm fixin' to cry
I'm fixin' to cry

Misfortune Has Reappeared

There's been some mistake here
misfortune has reappeared
Your timing is off
Look into my eyes
Can't you see
I'm no longer in love with you

Take your heartbreaking ways
Do what you do
Be the dream that you're dreaming of
I'm a dreamer too . . .
One is enough

Love, love, love
love, love, love
love, love, love
Don't shed your light on me now
Just leave me alone
Don't bring your promises here
No one is listening
Don't show me the dance that you'll do
or the cuddling to get your own way
I don't want to dry your tears of laughter or sorrow
I'm not the passionate kind
filled with tomorrows

Can't Keep Coming Home

I could say a thousand words to you
Most of them would probably come out wrong
I could tell you a thousand dreams I have
I wonder, would you want to belong

I can't keep coming home
waiting for you not to be loving someone new
I can't keep writing songs
to a lady who makes me weary

I've been telling you for quite some time
I won't be back some day
I've been telling you
I'll be gone
Woman, is that what you want

I can't keep coming home
waiting for you not to be loving someone new
I can't keep writing songs
to a lady who makes me weary

I could say I run with you through the forest
but I'm only trying to catch the wind
I could hold you in the coolness of the winter
but when I wake up
you're nowhere to be found

I can't keep coming home
waiting for you not to be loving someone new
I can't keep writing songs
for a lady who makes me weary

Don't Lie to Me

Don't lie to me
Don't lie to me
Don't tell me tales
Don't lie to me

When I first met you
everything came alive
for the first time

You were my sunshine
You chased all my clouds away
I loved you

Don't lie to me
Don't lie to me
Don't tell me tales
Don't lie to me

I feel just like the sea
Taking that ship to that port
and bringing it back again
I've been so many times before
I just don't want to be the sea
anymore

I just don't want to be alone
anymore

II

II

My Drinkin' Days Are Over
(but my nights have just begun)

The barroom sure is quiet
on this lonely Friday night
The jukebox plays another sad, sad song
written 'bout you and me
The pool balls are just a-settin' there
shinin' under the light
Barkeep, bring another whiskey
You're my only friend in sight

My drinkin' days are over
but my nights have just begun
Until I find another sweet little woman
to call my very own

My drinkin' days are over
but my nights have just begun
Until the mornin' light
me and ol' Jack
are sure gonna have some fun

Where are all those women
I used to see when you were around
Makin' eyes
tellin' lies
dreamin' up a storm

Darlin', you must have been gettin' yours
while I was gettin' mine
When I came home from work today
everything was gone

My drinkin' days are over
but my nights have just begun
Until the mornin' light
me and ol' Jack
are sure gonna have some fun

Until the mornin' light
me and ol' Jack
are sure gonna have some fun

I Don't Cry Those Tears

Those wide open spaces they've got me
The howling of the lone wolf is my song
A single campfire light
out on a moonlit night
is all this lonesome cowboy needs

And when the morning comes
it will be time for movin' on
I'll follow the sun another day
Not carin' where I go
I'm searching for old El Paso
I hear there's high dollars on the rodeo

I don't cry those tears the way I used to
or lay awake at night and wonder why
You left me for that gamblin' man who used you
and lost you in a game whose stakes weren't high

I don't cry those tears the way I used to
So if you love someone who can't be satisfied
just saddle up your pony one clear morning
and ride off to greet the coming night

Packin' Up Goin' Away

I'm packin' up
goin' away
Where I'm going I just can't say
Well I, just might go down Bermuda way
Grass skirts and gin rickeys all day

The autumn's come
the autumn's gone
Winter's here
and it stays so long
I just feel as though I've got to move
but I'll be back in four or five moons

I got some wine
some reefer too
And if you'd like
you can come too
We'll just sing and dance all day
And in the nighttime
the stars will take our place

White sand between my toes
Hearing stories the ocean knows
while I, kick back and watch the waves roll in
Feelin' so good
tomorrow I'll do it again

Peppermint Chick Blues

Gotta find me a woman soon
before I lose my mind
Gotta find me a skinny little lady
who wants to spend some time
Is there anyone a-listenin'
who's nice and skinny and who likes to sin
Come on   come on   come on

Gotta find me a roommate
who likes to boogie late
Gotta find me a partner
who won't say wait
Is there anyone a-listenin'
who's nice and anxious and who likes to sin
Come on   come on   come on

Gotta find me some sugarcane
who's as sweet as rain
Gotta fine me a peppermint chick
with something sweet that I can lick
Is there anyone a-listenin'
who's nice and sweet and who likes to sin
Come on   come on   come on

I Cried and I Cried

When I saw you dancing across from me
in that big, big dance hall
I had to take it upon myself
to ask you for the next waltz

When you placed your arms around my neck
and your head upon my shoulder
I went off into space somewhere
and I have not yet returned

Well I cried and I cried and I cried when you left me
and now it's so good to see you again
I've known and I've known and now I know it again
It's time for a lover to turn into a friend

We danced for a while and I left for a while
I said that I would come back
And when I came back I was a-lookin' for you
and when I found you you were lookin' for me

We went downtown to a country bar
and sat in a booth all alone
To this day I remember those kisses
Everyone would knock me off my feet

Well I cried and I cried and I cried when you left me
and now it's so good to see you again
I've known and I've known and now I know it again
It's time for a lover to turn into a friend

Oh the night it was grand and the breeze was just fine
as I held you close to me
Surrounded by tall buildings but they could not match
the height of my love for you
Thirty days of love like I've never known it
and I don't expect to again
One month of dreams come true
and good morning I love you
vanished like a shooting star

Well I cried and I cried and I cried when you left me
and now it's so good to see you again
I've known and I've known and I know it again
It's time for a lover to turn into a friend

It's time for a lover to turn into a friend

It's time for a lover
to turn
into
a
friend

That Time Will Never Come

I wish I
could see you one more time
Watch the wind blow through your hair once more
But I know
that time will never come

I wish I could see you smile again
I wish I could hold your hand once again
But I know
that time will never come

I wish I could kiss your lips once more
I wish I could caress your breast once again
But I know
that time will never come

Tears in Your Eyes

I've been through so many changes
Enough to know
there's more to come

Arranging
and then rearranging
Trying to let everything be

I once met some good mountain people
who showed me a new way of life
I made one more journey
back to the city
I came back to make you my wife

You told me
you had a new lover
You told me not to worry
You told me
you were confused
You told me
with tears in your eyes

The Southside of Blue

Sometimes
this life
can be
so sad

Sometimes
this life
can be
so sad

My friends Lord, they gone
the cup had done run dry
My friends Lord, they gone
the cup had done run dry

this is
this is
this is
the south side of blue

III

One More Time

One more time
love comes knocking at my door
One more time
things this time they feel for sure
A quiet beginning
I felt the warmth of a young new heart
She had her fire burning
She just had to take part

I took her by my side
as the zombie stalked the late night movie
I held her in my arms
and she kissed me
and I knew it was a long time coming
I knew it was a long time coming
But now I know
waiting's worth the time
Now I believe I know . . .
waiting for you babe
waiting's worth the time

It's late in the evening
Summer's just around the bend
City lights are turning
Hot cars race to beat the red
I walk the streets and I'm alone at night
Through the alleys and the shadows that I fight
In the distance there's a bedroom light
your image comes to mind

He's gonna take her by his side
as the zombie stalks the late night alleyway
He held her in his arms
and she kissed him
and I knew it was a long time coming
I knew it was a long time coming
But now I know
waiting's worth the time
Now I believe I know . . .
waiting for you babe
waiting's worth the time
waiting's worth the time
I believe I know . . .
I believe I know . . .

Good Thing

I've got a good thing
The way she do me
the way she do

She treat me like a real man
She give me that little thing

I've got a good thing
Not too tall
she's a skinny thing

She treat me like a real man
She give me that little thing

She's All Right, She's All Right

She's got a great big top
a skinny little middle
The hips on the girl
they sure like to wiggle
She's all right
She's all right, she's all right

She got long, long legs
people singing 'bout
A curvy shape
people talking 'bout
She's all right
She's all right, she's all right

She got eyes like diamonds
teeth like pearls
She kiss me slow
my heart goes a-whirl
She's all right
She's all right, she's all right

When the bars close down
and it's time to go home
sorry boys, I got to go
I can't stay for one more
I ain't got the time
My baby's callin'
She got lovin' on her mind
She's all right
She's all right, she's all right
She's all right, she's all right
She's all right, she's all right

Sure Do Me Fine

I've been out here on this highway
for such a long, long time
I've always traveled by myself
I've got a woman with me this time

It's not that I'm complaining
It's not that I'm bragging either
but in this Texas sun she sure looks fine
and I don't think right away that I'll leave her

She sure do me fine in the morning
She sure do me fine at night
She sure do me fine in the afternoon
She do me any time we think it's all right

Sometimes we get to talkin'
about lovers in the past
I might say something
that I know will get her
but it's only just for a laugh

Her brown eyes they get to sulking
she says she don't feel like talkin' no more
If we were living in a house in the city
you know she'd probably walk right out the door

She sure do me fine in the morning
She sure do me fine at night
She sure do me fine in the afternoon
She do me any time we think it's all right
She do me any time we think it's all right
She do me any time . . .
we think . . .
it's all right
it's all right
it's all right

I Like to Ride into the Sunset

(spoken by a man)
It's not that I don't love you
It's not as if I don't care
But I'm not ready to settle down
I'm havin' too much fun roamin' 'round

I like those wide open ranges
I like those star-filled nights
I like to ride into the sunset
I'm not ready for the love of a wife

(spoken by a woman)
You don't have to stay here
and keep me warm every night
Don't think for a minute
that my love for you
relies upon becoming your wife

So go ride those wide open ranges
I like those starry nights too
I'll wave as you ride into the sunset
And while you're gone
I'll be thinking of you

(together)
I like things just the way they are darlin'
Take care
because I love you

When You Jump

When you jump
you know you jump real high
When you jump
you know you jump real high
When you jump into my arms
I'll love you till the morning light

When you slip
slip slide across the floor
When you slip
slip slide across the floor
You can slip into my arms
from the evening to the morning dawn

When your naked
like a bluebird on the wire
When your naked
like a bluebird on the wire
With your skin so smooth
you set my little heart on fire

Went Walking with My Baby

I went walking with my baby
I went walking with my baby
I went walking with my baby
just the other day

We walked down to the corner
We walked down to the corner
We walked down to the corner
down by the stop sign

We stood there for a moment
We stood there for a moment
We stood there for a moment
and gazed into our eyes

I laid her down on my neighbor's lawn
I laid her down on my neighbor's lawn
I laid her down on my neighbor's lawn
right next to the tree

I spread apart my baby's lips
I stuck my tongue inside
I spread apart my baby's lips
I shot into the sky

I rolled her over on her belly
I rolled her over on her belly
I rolled her over on her belly
and then I turned her on her back again

Cannot Be Satisfied

There is a woman in my life
she bend over backwards
I'm not accustomed to this satin grace
I'm not accustomed to this fine lace

She cook me meals
She always happy
Even though I cannot be
I get worse by the day it seems
Someday she will leave me

I am a lonely man, aren't we all
I get something I like I do not like
I cannot be satisfied
come the rain or come the shine

You see the stars they are alone but connected
I am the line in between you cannot see
I see her walking up the road
I wish that I was not so

Don't Sing the Blues Today Smile

You say you got a problem with the rising sun
don't turn your face away
You say you got a problem with the bird's sweet voice
listen to what he say

Don't sing the blues today smile
Don't sing the blues today smile
Lay in your bed
kick off your shoes
relax for a while

You say you got a problem with your broken heart
you're afraid to let it heal
You say you got a problem with your long hairdo
I can't say as I know how you feel

You say you came home early from work one day
surprised to find your wife
Layin' in bed with her clothes on the floor
loving your best friend's wife

Don't sing the blues today smile
Don't sing the blues today smile
Jump in your bed
kick off your shoes
and relax for a while

Worried Blues

These worried blues
got me
like they never had me before
You see my baby gone and packed her case
I wonder will she be back through the door

The other night we argued
I called her a bitter name
I had the blind-eye in my system
and the devil he was playin' my game

Well I'm worried
Yes, I'm worried
I got them old worried blues
You see she was a good gal, Lord
One gal I sure hate to lose

Sittin' Here Supper's Done

Sittin' here
supper's done
Waitin' on her
Is she gonna come?

I don't know

Been waitin' for this day to come
Finally found the road I'm on
Is she gonna come?

I don't know

I used to be a crazy man
Always held an ace in hand
Since you left me babe
I've been losin'

I . . .
I don't know
Maybe it's better off this way

Things Have Been Stormy

Things have been stormy now for quite some time
Bein' followed 'round by that old north wind
My body screams for resting while my mind says to move on
The search for that rainbow of love goes on

Seems like
every time
I fall in love
I lose a piece of my mind

Oh Lord when you bring the next one around
bring her 'round slowly
let her
feel her ground
I'm not even close to bein' a mean old man
If-in I was well I could
understand

Seems like
every time
I fall in love
I lose a piece of my mind

Why Is It

She came in
through the kitchen door
Said hello to my friend, she didn't
say no more

Why is it
we can't get along
Why is it
we just keep moving on
Why is it
we can't get away
Tell me why is it
we just can't get along

She walked on through
the bedroom door
She took off all her clothes
She laid her body
on down next to mine
How was I to know

Why is it
we can't get along
Why is it
we just keep moving on
Why is it
we can't get away
Tell me why is it
we just can't get along
tell me why
why

Vanishing Affair

Sometimes living is easy
Sometimes it gets so hard
When you've got no one to turn to
nowhere to go
Sometimes it gets so hard

Turn up the music
I feel like dancing
Turn down the lights
I feel like romancing

I wait here in this forest
trying to see the light in between
Sheltering myself from the storms that herald my mind
It's a vanishing affair

IV

Baby Please

Baby please,
please don't leave me now
Baby please,
please don't leave me now
Things are just feeling all right
Please don't leave me now

Baby please,
spend one more night with me
Baby please,
just spend one more night with me
I'll call you a cab in the morning
Please spend one more night with me

I've been drunk and lonely
for almost twenty years
I thought things would change
when you walked in here
We seemed so good together
nobody foolin' 'round
Three months later
and you say you're leaving town

Baby please,
please don't leave me now
Baby please,
please don't leave me now
Things are just feelin' all right
Please don't leave me now

Lonely Cowboy

I don't know why I have this outlook
on things the way I do
I don't know why things always look bad
I always end up singing the blues
I guess I'm just lonely cowboy
I got them lonely cowboy blues

I wake up in the morning and I feel kind of empty
so I try to go back to sleep
I toss and I turn
I roll around a few times
I guess I caught all of my winks
I guess I'm just a lonely cowboy
I got them lonely cowboy blues

You know sometimes I wish I could fly
I wish I was a one of them birds
And there's other times I wish I could die
and move onto that other world
I guess I'm just a lonely cowboy
I got them lonely cowboy blues

For thirteen days and fourteen nights
I roamed the desert plains
I went searching for love
but it just wasn't there
I might just as well have searched for rain
I guess I'm just a lonely cowboy
I got them lonely cowboy blues

Morning Sun

I can think of almost everything
I'd like to say to you
I've said it to myself so many times
from the morning to the night's blue moon
Sometimes I still laugh
at some crazy things we've done
But it's been so long, it's been so long

You know all of the times I spent out on the road
I kept thinking of that girl back home
It kinda kept me goin'
and it kinda made me stop and wonder
You know I really wish I wasn't alone

Take me down to the beach
and toss me to those a-lake a-waters
Let me see you turning brown
from the heat of the mother sun
Let me rub down your body
and soothe any ache that you might have
Let me throw away your past
and we'll start a new day
with the morning sun
the morning sun

Riding through the fields on a horse christened Shotgun
Screamin' and hollerin'
shouting at the top of my voice
Feeling the wind on my face
is a favorite past time of mine
But it's been so long, it's been so long

Each morning I greet the new day
like the pedals of a rose
I open to the sun
and all of its splendor
You know I really wish
I'd find me a home

My Tears Are Falling Now

I never should have started this whole thing
I never should have let you go
I only thought we needed room to breathe
I didn't think things would go this far

I never thought that you would find a new love
I never thought that you'd be sleeping with someone
so soon

I tried to write you letters of love
I tried to keep me
in your mind
It didn't feel like things had gotten
so far out of hand

My tears are falling now
I never should have let you leave my side
My heart is breaking now
I never should have let you take that ride

Every Morning I Wake Up

Every morning I wake up
I go down to the river
to fetch me some water

I dunk my head far down under
and dream
of mermaids and pirates on the sea

I'm a restless kind of person
who doesn't like to see things
turning out the way they're turning out to be

I shall claim some land some day
and fight to keep it free for my children
They shall not be intervened
by all your social extremities

I'm a lover of one-hundred years ago
and how I came to be, in this day and age I'll never know

I hear friends talk of friends
To my ears
complaints come rushing in
like full-moon waves
I see young men leave their ladies at home
while they stalk the night for prey
Well, I hope they realize—that their future fortune lies
heavily upon what they give and take
today
today
what they give and take
today

V

You Came in the Morning

You came in the morning
and you wondered if it was all right
if you came in for a while

It was so good to see you
I was so surprised

I want to tell you
I like you a real lot

"Can I lay down next to you," you said
"I left you a note in the doorway.
I didn't think you heard me knocking."

You know this is crazy
I still can't believe this is happening to me
to me

I want to tell you
I like you a real lot
And you left before the sun came up

I'm Gonna Get to See My Baby

I'm gonna get to see my baby, (gonna get to see my baby)
I'm gonna get to see my baby, (gonna get to see my baby)
I'm gonna get to see my baby
in just a few more days

I'm gonna hug her when I see her
I'm gonna kiss her when I see her
I'm gonna squeeze her when I see her
I'm gonna be so pleased to see her
I'm gonna jump all up and down
We gonna ride all over this town

Well you might think I'm crazy
maybe a fool
but there's one thing I know
I'm gonna feel so cool

I'm gonna get to see my baby, (gonna get to see my baby)
I'm gonna get to see my baby, (gonna get to see my baby)
I'm gonna get to see my baby
in just a few more days

She's a little on the skinny side but that's all right with me
She's a little on the tall side but that's all right with me
As long as she's by my side Wednesday afternoon by three

What are you going to tell her?
I'm gonna tell her that I love her
What are you going to say?
You're beautiful baby
What are you going to do?
I'm gonna take her to that Breezeway Motel
I'm gonna stay on the girl
till way past the hour of twelve

I'm gonna get to see my baby, (gonna get to see my baby)
I'm gonna get to see my baby, (gonna get to see my baby)
I'm gonna get to see my baby
in just a few more days

My Baby Says She Loves Me

My baby says she loves me
and I know the reason why
My baby says she loves me
and I know the reason why
She got a diamond on her hand
and a house sittin' way up high

My baby says she loves me
and I know the reason why
My baby says she loves me
and I know the reason why
She got a brand new car
and a pile o' dough a mile high

My baby . . . loves me . . .
and I know the reason why
My baby . . . loves me . . .
and I know the reason why
She got everything she need
and that's the reason why

My Kind of Woman

She love me
She hate me
She love to forsake me
She cut me wide open
My heart lie there bleeding
She push me
She shove me
She force me to love her
Oh, oh   oh, oh
she's my kind of woman

She rob me
She beat me
She love to deceive me
My friends all stay clear
The mean things they hear
Screaming in public
She need me in private
Oh, oh   oh, oh
she's my kind of woman

Snakebite

You take all my money
You stay out all night
You bring me your troubles
Well don't it suit you right

I'm tired of weeping
and drinking myself drunk
I'm tired of dreaming
of your so-called love

So I went downtown
It was just the other night
Down to Shakey's Place
It was a real hot night

I ordered some bourbon
and a glass of beer
I ordered another
I turned and saw you there

Back in the corner
Legs crossed and all
With a mule-faced buck skinner
I'm a snakebite
I'm a snakebite
I'm a snakebite

Goodbye Baby

Goodbye baby
Goodbye baby got to go
Goodbye baby
Goodbye baby got to go
Don't worry 'bout me darlin'
knockin' on your door no more

I'll see ya darlin'
Maybe I'll see you someday
I'll see ya darlin'
Maybe I'll see you someday
And when I do baby
I hope some things are goin' your way

I'm gonna start up my Chevy
Lay some rubber in all four gears
I'm gonna start up my Chevy
Lay some rubber in all four gears
I'm down the road darlin'
Someone else can dry your tears

VI

Black Bill Blues

Razor Face, Razor Face
don't do you no good to race
Me and you both know you just slow

Razor Face
laser pace
never heard of can't relate
Smilin' all the time in coca space

Old Black Bill he shufflin' laundry
boilin' steak at lunch in water
Make us laugh all through the day

Tellin' tales of gamblin' weekends
Flashin' wads of money in my eyes
Doin' LSD
and goin' down inside

Got a smilin' girl
she nice and skinny
Cook me meals
now ain't that funny
A year ago
I was quite schizoid

She walk by me pinch my belly
Say she like to come along
Give me my night shirt
put on your
mornin' gown

When the Morning Comes

When the morning comes
I'll be gone
When the morning comes
baby I'll be gone
It's not a big decision
don't know why it took so long

When the sun gets up, over the trees
When the sun gets up, over the trees
Gonna set my sails up high and catch onto that breeze

Baby won't you please come
Gonna miss you so
Baby won't you please come
You'll never know
I'm gonna load up the pickup and go right past Buffalo

Don't know how I met ya, but I was fortunate
Don't know how I met ya, but I'll never forget ya
You're something that's with me every minute of every day

Darlin' when you kiss me
you know I lose my mind
Baby when you squeeze me
I know you're mine
I never met nobody like you nowhere any time

You're my sugar-bear babe
My sweet-bun delight
My frosted éclair
I love every bite
I'm lonely in the morning, wake up, you're not by my side

By the Water

For quite some time now
you've been telling me
that you're leaving
I've been sitting on the edge of my chair
saying please, please, please
don't go

I've been lying in bed
twisting my head
trying to figure out how to please you
All I hear are your troubles and fears
and why all of your lovers leave you

I'm not going to take it no more
I'm afraid I've got to head for the door
For there's someone waiting by the water
with a smile and a kiss hello
Someone waiting by the water
glistening in the sun

All of the good times that we shared
have long since disappeared
And to think that things could change in time
is just a crazy thought inside my mind
Your losing makes me feel like I'm losing all the time

For there's someone waiting by the water
with a smile and a kiss hello
Someone waiting by the water
glistening in the sun

Who's That Boy

Who's that boy I saw you standing with today
Your eyes were lit up with that love-look I used to see
Hand in hand you walked along the shoreline at sunset
What's the matter baby, don't you like me anymore
I said, "Ooo, Ooo, Ooo."

I saw you kiss him and hold him in your arms
He pressed his hands into you back
you moved around for more
Silhouettes have been known not to tell the truth
So I moved up closer to you babe
so I could hear your breath
You said, "Ooo, Ooo, Ooo."

What's the matter baby, don't you like me anymore
Have my stories all grown old
Are my ways just a bore
What's the matter baby, don't you think that I'm still nice
Don't you think I'm still good lookin', baby didn't you think twice
I say, "Ooo, Ooo, Ooo."

Almost Took My Life

Yes I've had the blues before
I caught them down the road one time
Oh yes I've had the blues before
I caught them down the road one time
The poor girl she broke my heart
She broke my heart, yes it's true

That little girl you know
I thought she was my friend
That little girl you know
I thought she was my friend
I almost took my life
Oh, what a fool I would have been

VII

It Took Me a Long Time

It took me a long time
I must admit it's true
To get beyond this point of stagnation
To
get rid of you

Every time I'd find a new lover
you'd come around to me
Sweet talkin', fancy hip walkin'
layin' your line on me

Well you can keep right on talkin'
Keep right on walkin'
'cause I'm
not gonna pay no mind to you

I'd just be gettin' warmed up
Having lots of fun
It'd be good not to see you hangin' 'round
I'd be sure we were done
And then you'd come around with that look in your eye
towin' me over to you
You'd be
Sweet talkin', fancy hip walkin'
layin' your line on me

Well you can keep right on talkin'
Keep right on walkin'
'cause I'm
not gonna pay no mind to you

The Train Song

Train come 'round the corner
goin' to take me away
Train come 'round the corner
goin' to take me away
My mamma don't love me
and my papa don't want me to stay

Woman done left me
for another man
Woman done left me
for another man
I gave her everything
I just don't understand

Goin' down to Orleans
learn to play the blues
Yes, I'm goin' down to Orleans
learn to play the blues
After losin' you, babe
I got nothin' to lose

7:45
hear that whistle blow
It's 7:45
hear that whistle blow
Fifteen more minutes
I'll think of you no more

She's a cool streamliner
with a ragin' smokestack
She's a cool streamliner
with a ragin' smokestack
I got a ticket in my hand
and a tilt to my top hat

Mr. Conductor
load my baggage please
Mr. Conductor
won't you load my baggage please
I got a gig to play
I'm goin' down to New Orleans

VIII

Song for Mindy

She tells me that she loves me
Says she wants to be mine
She says that she will wait for me
While I go out to find
She says that she wishes
I were nicer to her
It's not hard to believe her
I can see it in her eyes

You ...
truly do love me
Nobody else has ever tried
You ...
truly do love me
Nobody else
has ever taken the time

Maybe someday soon
we can spend some time together
Maybe someday real soon
we can go away together

Woman in this World

Is there a woman in this world
who doesn't need life's finer things
Is there a woman in this world
who doesn't need life's finer things
I'd give her my last dollar
and a small, thin golden ring

Is there a woman in this world
who doesn't need to fuss and fight
Is there a woman in this world
who doesn't need to fuss and fight
I'd find a hundred dollars
We'd paint the town blue tonight

Is there a woman in this world
who only needs one man for life
one woman
one man
Is there a woman in this world
who only needs one man for life
I'd find a million dollars
and buy her everything in sight

I Really Do Love You

A while ago
I was out looking for a friend to play some music
I found him
and right next door
there was a lady whose presence caught me by surprise
by surprise

She was the wind to me
She was looking for a lover
and so was I
so was I

And I listened
She seemed to know just what she was talking about
She had a way about her you couldn't mistake

After a week of seeing her
and trying to kiss her lips
we ended up alone
making love
making love

She was telling me things
I'd forgotten all about
She became a friend of mine
I'd been really insecure about love
for such a long, long time

It takes me so long to meet someone
and when I do
it seems as though there's just not enough time
not enough time

I get to talking and rambling on
about all the wrong things
Is it really too late
Are you're going to leave me
leave me my friend
I really do love you

Love is Broken

You've taken all of my love
and kept it to yourself
You've tried to keep me hidden
from the ladies that are my friends

I feel our love has taken
up permanent ownership
I feel our love is broken
I never wanted this

You can call me
anytime you like
You will always be
a lover of my life

IX

Treated and Released

You call me like a lover
in desperate need of a friend
Your body trembles slightly
and you shiver in the cold
You tell me you've been thinking
of a land that's far away
and baby,
just the two of us
on a hilltop far away

I don't think so baby
Your love was just a passing thing
I don't think so baby
You and me just weren't meant to be

You're a crier and a liar
You've been through the pimps
Face busted, bruised, battered, beaten, shattered, torn
I'm not your savior
I'm no longer the new boy next door
Take your love to another full-time loser
I'm looking for my own quiet space in the center of the city
I'm looking for my own
I've been treated and released

Rip Them Chains

Never been much
for falling in love
Never been much
for that personal touch
Never seem to keep
one baby at a time
Never seem to keep my hands
away from that stuff

Maybe you know what I'm talking about
Maybe you, you're just like me

You gotta
touch that stuff
You gotta
kiss those lips
You gotta rip them chains
You gotta censor out the pain

I Know You (Little Cutie)

Little Cutie just to look at you
I wouldn't think that you're lonely too
You wanna dance?
Fat chance

You like the booze
I know you
You like to choose
I know you
Don't like to lose
I know you
You like to run the show

You look so fragile
in your Chinese shoes
Don't like to drive fast
you might get abused
Remember me
I'm still looking at you

Oh my God
she's approaching me
What will I do now
I'm starting to freeze
What can I do
try to move over
She walked right by
SHE DIDN'T EVEN NOTICE!

You walk so tall in your designer jeans
Ridin' bronco
sometimes ain't what it seems
Your see-through shirt
was in one of my dreams

Oh my God
she's approaching me
What will I do now
I'm starting to freeze
What can I do
try to move over
She walked right by
SHE DIDN'T EVEN NOTICE!

Temptation

Walking through this jungle
bare feet and short sleeves
Broken champagne glasses
checks and open letters
Night will soon be falling
It falls so hard around you now
Temptation
is calling

Who was that you saw
walking by your window
You talk you talk you talk
no one is listening

YOU SPILL YOURSELF OUT!
half the room is empty
Temptation
is calling

Every morning it's harder
to pull yourself together
To look your friends, look them in the eye
Thinking maybe you're no good

You get farther and farther
inside yourself
You can't talk to no one
MAYBE YOU SHOULD TURN YOURSELF IN!
MAYBE YOU JUST CAN'T WIN!

Don't Call Me

You keep on saying that your world is spinning
you don't know which way to turn
Your heart brings tears to your eyes
your eyes drip onto the phone
Your voice it cracks like a stone on glass
'cause we both know what's going down
Yes we both know what's going down
We both know
what's
going down

I could hear your laughter in the middle of the night
you're so many miles away
I'm still connected to your heart somehow
but soon I'm gonna cut myself away
away
away
I'm gonna cut myself away

They say
that the first love is the roughest
I'm telling you
I just don't think it's true

They say
that the first love is the roughest
I'm telling you
I just don't think it's true

Don't call me till your world stops spinning
Don't call me till
you
stop
falling down

They say
that the first love is the roughest
I'm telling you
I just don't think it's true

They say
that the first love is the roughest
I'm telling you
I just don't think it's true

Don't call me till your world stops spinning
Don't call me till
you
stop
falling
down

Break My Heart

It's late in the night
I've been waiting for you to show
Everyone that's come through those doors
has looked a lot like you
It's all this torment
that you put me through
Those sudden calls of danger
You need to see me now
You're not going to take my heart this time
You're not going to break my heart this time

It's a long way home
in the stillness of this seasoned air
The feelings that I'd hoped for
seem so far away

Chancing on the phone to ring
knowing what you'd say
The sleepless nights
a worried daze
you do it every time

You're not gonna take my heart this time
You're not gonna break my heart this time
You're not gonna take my heart
You're not gonna break my heart
You're not gonna take my heart this time

X

Wine and Roses

In the days of wine and roses
laughter filled the air
In the days of the old-time movies
things were so much fun
In the morning the sun would shine
through the window on your face
In the evening the moon would caress us
in love's embrace

But now the wine has all been drunk
and the roses are no more
And the laughter that filled the air
has been covered with the sound of crying
And the movies we used to share
are spent by looking through the crowd
Gone before the sunrise
back before the moon shine

I know you've heard this
once or twice from me
It's an old song and dance routine
that I used to do for you
I would say that I love you
You would shyly hide your face
I thought that's all I had to do
to keep things in place

Now I know, there's more than words involved
I swear I know what it takes
to make a lady feel in love
all her heart can take
I can't forget the wine and the roses
I can't forget the old-time movies
Can't forget the sun and the moon
Throw out that old song and dance routine

If you don't mind
me being in love with you
for just a little while longer
If you don't mind me holding on to you
for just a little while,
just a little while longer,
I will

Oh the Way

Oh the way
you look to me
What words can I speak
that might turn your love to me
What can I buy you
knowing money can't buy love
What can I show you

Early morning
dew is falling
You lie unbroken
shattered dreams
Castle on the hilltop
you warrior's down below
leading his men
as hell unfolds

You call out his name
he is so far away
You hear the firing
You hear the screaming
You see the smoke and the dust
in the twilight's gleaming
You fear for fire and lust
rampant in the village

Oh the way, you look to me
What words can I speak
that might turn your love to me
What can I buy you
knowing money can't buy love
What can I show you

The Nights Are Long

The nights are long and filled with pain
I'm not too strong should I remain

You're all so vicious
you're so unkind
Is this the truth
am I losing my mind

I liked your moves
I fell too fast
A sensuous miss
You moved too fast

The stories told were all untrue
and so my life gets tied in knots of blue

I know yourself
and your next play
The break away
the search for day

You've never known to be alone
You're not yourself, the tone I know

I'm leaving soon
for the western road
Your openness will warm the cold

There's types of life
you'll find, I've found
that bypass objects
take off your crown

Give Your Heart Away

If you think there's no love here
If for some reason things are unclear
Don't turn your head and look to the ground
Please remember how it feels
when there's no one around

When you wake up and the sun's not shining
and the fields are filled with the mist in your eyes
When the strangers on the road look good to you
your new love is just up ahead

Give your heart away (don't be afraid)
Give your love away (don't sit and wait)
In the heat of the evening (give your heart away)
There's a sense of completing
the puzzle of love in your heart

When the wind is the voice of your only friend
whistling your favorite songs in the night
You try not to hear but the message gets louder
You must remember how it feels
when there's no one around

Give your heart away (don't be afraid)
Give your love away (don't sit and wait)
In the heat of the evening (give your heart away)
There's a sense of completing
the puzzle of love in your heart
When there's no one around
When there's no one around
No one around

Killin' Blues

Oh Lord let me live just one more day
Oh Lord let me live just one more day
It's just not fair dear Father
to give a boy the blues this way

Fill me with pain, Lord
with the cryin' of the children
Fill me with pain, Lord
with the cryin' of the children
Just bring the sun up one more time
before this man's killin'

Let me see the sun, Lord
hear the people down below
Let me see the sun, Lord
hear the people down below
And when the sun sinks behind the hill
I know it will be my time to go

XI

Poor Man

I'm just a poor man
I got nobody to make me feel good
I'm just a poor man
I got nobody to make me feel good
I got no place to call my home
I'm in this world
I'm all alone

I got no color
no change money to keep me fed
I got no color
no change money to keep me fed
I got no place to call my home
I'm in this world
I'm all alone

Hey Brother

Hey brother
have you seen the one I love
Hey brother
have you seen the one I love
When I woke up this morning
everything she owned was gone

Hey brother
can you spare some change
or maybe just a sip of your wine
You got a cigarette
The landlord comes tomorrow
and I'm down on my luck once again

Hey sister
have you got a place in your heart
Tell me sister
have you got a place in your heart—for me
I never knew my father
and my family
has turned their backs on me

I'm cold
and I'm all alone
Yes, I'm cold
and I'm all alone
I guess I'll catch a ride
to the other side of town

Ain't Got No Money

I ain't got no money
I'm as broke as any man could be
I ain't got no money
I'm as broke as any man could be
Why'd you have to go woman
and make a fool out of me

I've lost all hope
and my faith is too blind to see
I've lost all hope
and my faith is too blind to see
Why'd you have to go woman
and make a fool out of me

You used to treat me so kind
You used to treat me so nice

When I first met you
you said everything would be all right
You'd stay right here
and keep me warm
every night

Now your gone
You're never home
You see me on the street
you say, "Leave me alone!"
I shoulda quit you babe
such a long, long time ago
Then I wouldn't be worried
wouldn't be worried no more

Hello

Hello
how you doin'
It's good to see you again

Hello
how you doin'
It's good to see you old friend
I see your smile
in my mind
now and then

Went up to Wellesley Island
'bout a month ago
Met a pretty woman there
well I guess I should have known
All those fish in the sea
they ain't lookin' for a home

Goin' Home

I'm goin' home
to where I used to be
I'm goin' home
to where I used to be
I'm gonna walk to the porch door
see who remembers me

I'm gonna call my baby
let the telephone ring
I'm gonna call my baby
let the telephone ring
If a new man answer
I guess she found another thing

I'm goin' down to the corner
where the boys used to hang
I'm goin' down to the corner
where the boys used to hang
I'm gonna get myself a pistol
somebody's goin' down tonight

XII

She Can Boogaloo

There's a funny little girl lives on my block
She got funny lookin' legs and she laughs a lot
She got one brown eye and one of them blue
but boy oh boy can she boogaloo

I loves that girl
Yes, I loves that girl
It don't matter to me that she can barely see
there's more important things in life to me
Yes, I loves that girl

She's a short little thing
about four foot eleven
Just as wide as she's tall, oh good heaven
She eat like a horse
look like a cow that go moo
but boy oh boy can she boogaloo

Yes, I loves that girl
I loves that girl
It don't matter to me that she can barely see
there's more important things in life to me
Yes, I loves that girl

Now you know 'bout my baby
tell me 'bout yours
Is she everything you dreamed of
maybe more
Does she treat you like a king
does she do what you do
More important, does she boogaloo

I loves that girl
Yes, I loves that girl
It don't matter to me that she can barely see
'cause there's more important things in life to me
Yes, I loves that girl
Come here baby
Gimme some of that good stuff

XIII

Cryin' Cat Blues

There's a cat crying out my window
The noise of the traffic is steady
The dogs bark below and aside
The blue light shows shadows
as I sit clean of wrap
and I think to myself
as I sing to myself
as I rode by myself
past your house
So late the moonlight
So free I feel
I've never felt

It Was Love

Sunshine
in my life since the day
I turned I heard you laugh
saw the smile on your face
It was love

Seen the joy and dried
the sorrows of your tears
And in my time
you've done the same for me

It was love
oh   oh   it was love

We held each other's hands
and danced in the rain
And since that day you gave your love
I've never been the same

it was love
Oh   oh   it was love

We held each other's hands
and danced in the rain
And since that day you gave your love
I've never been the same
Oh   oh   it was love
Oh   oh   it was love
Oh   oh   it was love

My Heart's on Fire

My heart's on fire
for your love
My heart's on fire
for your love

Oh won't you please
stand in my doorway
Oh won't you please
please take my hand
My heart's on fire
I'm takin' a stand

You are so pretty
like the mornin' sun
You are so beautiful
I'm glad you've cum

Oh won't you please
share with me laughter
Oh won't you please
please share with me
My heart's on fire
I'm takin' a stand

I Love My Baby

I love my baby like the river water love to run
I love my baby like I love the rays from the sun
She is the wind you know
changing direction all the time
She is the clouds you know
imaginary forms I see in the sky

My baby don't wear no tight dress
no perfume but her own
My baby don't wear no high heels
she leave well enough alone
My baby don't need no fancy man
to show off downtown
she don't need no diamond on her hand
to let you know she's around

Our love like the spring time
budding new life all the time
Our love like the stars in the sky
a path to follow for the weary at sea
She is the wind you know
her love is everywhere around
She is the universe
to me

She don't need to be told no tales
'cause she already knows
she don't need no leash around her collar
'cause she free to come and go
She don't need no Cadillac to drive to the corner and back
All she need is a loving man and I do what I can
I do what I can

Refried Beans

You don't have to tell me baby
where you're steppin' out tonight
You don't have to tell me baby
where you're steppin' out tonight
We've been together so long
I know everything will be all right

The food's in the Frigidaire
refried beans in the cupboard
The food's in the Frigidaire
refried beans in the cupboard
It's my night to stay home
while the girl goes out and plays

These girls are so crazy
They just keep goofin'
all night long
They primp
and they fuss
and they flirt with the boys
all night long
They have a real good time
I ain't worried 'bout her doin' me wrong

Ship Upon the Sea

My baby says she love me
love me every way
My baby say she love me
love me every way
Say it don't matter how many ways
just make sure you love me today

My baby is so pretty
pretty as the sea
My baby is so pretty
she's a pretty girl to me
When she love me I'm a nebula
or maybe I'm a ship on the bottom of the sea

My baby always happy
never make me sad
My baby satisfied
she never want what we do not have
She can stay as long as she want to
and when she don't want to
you know she can go

Good Country Lovin'

Seems like forty-seven years ago
I came out to these mountains
I was lookin' for gold
Got me a nice spot next to the river
where the fish were a-plenty
here I'll stay forever

Got me a wife from the town next door
We had one child
I said, "Let's have some more!"
So we did in fact
we had one baker's dozen
and we just blamed it on good country lovin'

Good country lovin' can do you no harm
Find yourself a partner that'll keep you warm
Good country lovin'
no it ain't bad
It's the best kind of lovin' I've ever had

Well Susie, that's my wife and me
we're prit'near now eighty-three
Now I know to a lot of you folks that's old
but to us it's more valuable than any of that gold
You see we found out one thing early in life
and I swear it'll always be right
You can live in the city and get computerized or move to the country and
realize

Good country lovin' can do you no harm
Find yourself a partner that'll keep you warm
Good country lovin'
no it ain't bad
It's the best kind of lovin' we've ever had

Baby Gone and Left Me

Baby gone and left me
she many miles away
says it won't be too long 'fore she
be back this way
I'm cryin'
Whoa you know I been cryin'
You know I can't please myself
She the only thing that keep me satisfied

Baby she been gone now for two or three days
Maybe it's a hundred
my mind's in a haze
I been cryin'
Whoa you know I been cryin'
You know I sure miss my candy
My sweet tooth ache every night

Superman

Some folks thinks I's a policeman
watching every move they make
Some folks thinks I's a policeman
watching every move they make
Where'd they get this business
Oh Lord, for heaven's sake

My baby thinks I'm Superman
says that I can do no wrong
My baby thinks I'm Superman
she says that I can do no wrong
Even though I'm small
she says that I'm big and strong

My mamma thinks I'll kill myself
my papa does too
My little brother told me so
what was I to do
I hate to disappoint the folks
tell me, what was I to do
I'm just a poor white boy
singin' these poor black blues

The blues is my life
so far nobody been right
I'm the only one that knows
that I'm doin' all right
I got the beat
Yes, I got the beat
You can talk all you want to people
but I think my baby's right

Sweet Christmas Love

It's good to see you darlin'
on this lovely Christmas Eve
Yes, it's good to see you darlin'
on this lovely Christmas Eve
You know the childrens is nestled all in their sleepy time
and visions of lovin' you is all that's on my mind

Chestnuts roasting on an open fire
outside the snow is falling down
Chestnuts roasting on an open fire
my love for you is tumbling down
You feel so good to me baby
I hope Santa's on the far side of town

The sleigh bells is ringin' long into the night
Come here one more time darlin'
let me hold you tight
There's a star in the sky baby
with its love light shinin' through
Come here my little sugar plum
let me make
sweet Christmas love to you

You bring joy to my world
and make all my holidays so merry
A sleigh ride in the moonlight
and a snifter right with sherry
Let's raise our glass in kind, and toast to Auld Lang Syne
'cause lovin' you baby,
lovin' you baby,
is all that's on this little elf's mind

XIV

Oh Darlin'

Oh darlin', won't you take a walk with me
Oh darlin', won't you take a walk with me
I'll give you more good loving
any girl ever need

Oh baby
please take ahold of my hand
Oh baby!
please take ahold of my left hand
I'll give you more good loving
any girl ever hope to understand

I'm gonna walk to the creek yard
be back before dawn
take you upstairs
and lay your body down
Baby!
be careful of the big man
I'll give you more good loving
any sweet thing ever hope to understand

I'm gonna take you downtown
to the back of Warren Street
where the Red Door used to swing
Charge all the peoples a dollar and a half
just to see you shake your thing
Baby!
be careful of the big man
(yeah, that be me baby)
I'll give you more good loving
any sweet thing ever hope to understand

Dig Me a Hole

I'm gonna dig me a hole in my backyard
till I can't see over the top
Dig me a hole in my backyard
till I can't see over the top
It's my own damn yard
I'll die right here if I want

I'm gonna cut down this tree
with my big ol' ax
let it fall where it may
I'm gonna cut down this tree
with my big ol' ax
let it fall where it may
It's my own damn yard
and I'll cut down what I want

I'm gonna build me
a party house
on the far corner down below
I'm gonna build me
a party house
on the far corner down below
It's my own damn yard
and I'll party all night if I want

I'm gonna get me a diamond shooter
six slugs loaded tall
I'm gonna get me a diamond shooter
six slugs loaded tall
It's my own damn yard
try and stop me and I'll watch you fall

Worried 'Bout My Baby

I'm worried, worried, my baby's gone away
I'm worried, worried, my baby's gone away
She's gone back to Texas
Lord, I hope she be back some day

I took her from her family
when she was just a little girl
I took her from her family
when she was just a little 19-year-old girl
I didn't always treat her right
There's worse men out there I'm sure

I'm worried 'bout my baby (worried 'bout my baby)
I'm worried 'bout my baby (worried 'bout my baby)
Worried 'bout my baby
I hope she be back some day

I'm cryin', cryin'
baby please come home
I'm cryin', cryin'
baby please come home
Don't stay down in Texas and leave me all alone

I'm worried 'bout my baby (worried 'bout my baby)
I'm worried 'bout my baby (worried 'bout my baby)
Worried 'bout my baby
I hope she be back some day

I Didn't Think You'd Go

Thinking back just a couple years
wondering where you are
I travel down that memory lane
every so often dear
I get to thinking 'bout the way things were
flowers blooming in the spring
I get to thinking 'bout those rainy times we shared

I didn't think
you'd go

Seeing you with your new man in white
made me feel rather ill
You know it made my actions
quite extraordinaire
I get to steer this old paddle boat
up and down this old river
and if you're standing on shore, you can hear . . .
yodelayee, yodelayee, oooo
yodelayee, yodelayee, oooo

I didn't think
you'd go

It's Been a Real Good Time

Train come
rollin' down the track
Yes, a train come
rollin' down the track
When the big train come
I won't be comin' back

Silver dollar
had done lost its shine
My shoes is thin
I done walked this town
When the big train come
you won't see me around

Well, hey, hey, hey
it's been a real good time
I said, hey, hey, hey, it's been a real good time
Now I got to move on
further on down the line

Said hey Big Stevie,
Mr. Harmonica Tom
Said hey Bobcat Jerry,
the Hawk he only fly at night
It's been a real good time
When the big train come
I got to move on down the line

Gary's Song
(to my good 'ol boy brother)

Just when you think you've felt it all
another hero begins to fall

And the one you've leaned against
is no longer there for you to call

It was so sad to see you go
in that fleeting moment's time

Another good ol' boy is gone
and now I'm closer to being alone

Oh those cigarettes you loved
for those decades on end
finally blackened you up
and took you away in one week's time

It truly is a crying shame

So many of your friends
they shed their tears
they toasted with your Pabst Blue Ribbon
and reminisced about the years

There will never be another
not that I will ever know
who laughed and spoke the truth
of everything he knew

www.ingramcontent.com/pod-product-compliance
Lightning Source LLC
Chambersburg PA
CBHW071758090426
42737CB00012B/1873